SELF-DIRECTED WORK TEAMS:
A PRIMER

Cresencio Torres
and
Jerry Spiegel

San Francisco

Copyright © 1990 by Jossey-Bass/Pfeiffer

ISBN: 0-88390-057-2
Library of Congress Catalog Card Number 91-42

Library of Congress Cataloging-in-Publication Data

Torres, Cresencio, 1947–
    Self-directed work teams: a primer/Cresencio Torres and Jerry Spiegel.
       p.   cm.
    Includes bibliographical references.
    ISBN 0-88390-057-2
    1. Work groups. I. Title.
HD66.T63   1991
658.4'036—dc20   91-42

Published by

350 Sansome Street, 5th Floor
San Francisco, California 94104-1342
(415) 433-1740; Fax (415) 433-0499
(800) 274-4434; Fax (800) 569-0443

Visit our website at: www.pfeiffer.com

Outside of the United States, Jossey-Bass/Pfeiffer products can be purchased from the following Simon & Schuster International Offices:

Jossey-Bass/Pfeiffer
3255 Wyandotte Street East
Windsor, Ontario N8Y 1E9
Canada
888-866-5559; Fax 800-605-2665

Prentice Hall Professional
Locked Bag 507
Frenchs Forest PO NSW 2086
Australia
61 2 9454 2200; Fax 61 2 9453 0089

Prentice Hall/Pfeiffer
P.O. Box 1636
Randburg 2125
South Africa
27 11 781 0780; Fax 27 11 781 0781

Prentice Hall
Campus 400
Maylands Avenue
Hemel Hempstead
Hertfordshire HP2 7EZ
United Kingdom
44(0) 1442 881891; Fax 44(0) 1442 882074

Simon & Schuster (Asia) Pte Ltd
317 Alexandra Road
#04–01 IKEA Building
Singapore 159965
Asia
65 476 4688; Fax 65 378 0370

Printing 10 9 8 7 6

    This book is printed on acid-free, recycled stock that meets or exceeds the minimum GPO and EPA requirements for recycled paper.

TABLE OF CONTENTS

PREFACE

Since the beginning of recorded history, people have been actively engaged in tasks directly related to maintaining their economic survival. Concerns such as the quality of work, the quantity of production, recognition, reward systems, leadership styles, and methods for organizing labor and work systems have been present in every organization, from ancient craft guilds to those in our present post-industrial information age. Today's organizations are still grappling to find the appropriate strategies for designing work. Even more important, organizations must find ways to educate and train their work forces to compete successfully against the rapidly expanding global market, to stay afloat in the face of deregulation, and to keep abreast of rapid technological change.

The implementation of and commitment to self-directed work teams can help organizations to meet this challenge. Self-directed work teams are empowered work groups that are committed to improving work processes and are concerned with the successful delivery of products that meet their customers' needs.

Organizations today are realizing that employees at all levels must be contributing, participating members of the work force in order to be competitive in the world marketplace. They are becoming aware that self-directed work teams offer many advantages over more traditional ways of organizing labor: skills and tasks are widely distributed among all team members;

teams are held accountable for maintaining and improving the processes for which they are responsible; and all team members share leadership and management responsibilities, which can reduce the number of supervisory personnel on the payroll and thereby cut costs.

Self-directed work teams create an environment that empowers the employees to contribute to the improvement of products and services by giving them the authority to improve the work itself. This environment can result in more satisfying jobs that offer employees greater challenge, variety, and opportunity for job enhancement.

The advent of self-directed work teams presents a unique opportunity for organizations to revolutionize their management and operational systems. Prerequisites for successful implementation include a new kind of leadership and a bold new attitude about how the work force can be organized. Effectively implemented, this leadership style will change the role of the supervisor and the way that work is managed. In some cases, it requires union participation and the renegotiation of certain organizational rules. It challenges traditional management philosophy, but it can contribute to the accomplishment of a very important goal: making workers feel like partners in their organizations.

The implementation of self-directed work teams in organizations is not only beneficial to employees but a smart business strategy as well. For example, workers organized in functional groups can get to know one another and develop mutual trust; and they can become more flexible, more quality conscious, and more committed to excellence in their work. Because self-directed work teams give employees the power to improve work methods and procedures, the organization sees an increase in product quality and quantity, and attrition rates improve. With all the challenges that organizations are facing today, the self-directed work team is a concept whose time has come.

INTRODUCTION

The purpose of this book is to educate HRD (human resource development) professionals, organization-development consultants, managers, and other interested employees about the concept of self-directed work teams. The information contained in this book is general enough to be applicable to most organizations; therefore, this book should be regarded as a primer for developing more effective organizations.

Chapter One defines the three principles that govern successful self-directed work-team systems and the specific processes that accompany each principle.

Chapter Two uses the analogy of the athletic team to describe five models that are appropriate for common work tasks. The models compare work teams to baseball, football, basketball, volleyball, and tennis teams and illustrate the concept that form must follow function if a person wishes to select the appropriate model.

Chapter Three explores four benefits that result from establishing successful work-team systems, illustrating how self-directed work teams contribute to increased productivity, consistent quality in customer service, increased employee morale, and reduced overhead.

Chapter Four defines the three key strategies and the three action steps essential to implementing successful self-directed work-team systems. In addition, the barriers to each action step and the processes for overcoming those barriers are presented.

Appendix 1 outlines a training program to support and enhance the implementation of a work-team system. Appendix 2 gives a historical overview of predominant systems of management.

This book is written for those individuals who are seeking innovation and change in the work place. The principles of self-directed work teams can be used by any organization that uses or is considering the use of work teams. Methods for implementing work-team systems will vary with each organization, but the basic tenets discussed in this book must be present in some form when making the transition.

CHAPTER 1

WHAT ARE SELF-DIRECTED WORK TEAMS?

Organize as much as possible around teams, to achieve enhanced focus, task orientation, innovativeness and individual commitment.
(Peters, 1987, p. 356)

A self-directed work team is a functional group of employees (usually between eight and fifteen members) who share the responsibility for a particular unit of production. The work team consists of trained individuals who possess the technical skills and abilities necessary to complete all assigned tasks. Management has delegated to the self-directed work team the authority to plan, implement, control, and improve all work processes (see Figure 1).

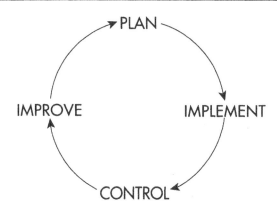

Figure 1. Authorities Delegated to Self-Directed Work Teams

Self-directed work teams are accountable for production, scheduling, quality, and costs; these responsibilities have been clearly defined in advance. Each team member possesses a variety of technical skills and is encouraged to develop new ones in order to increase job flexibility and value to the work team.

A typical self-directed work team would be responsible for monitoring and reviewing overall process performance, scheduling and inspecting its own work, assigning tasks to group members, solving problems, and improving work processes. Some self-directed work teams conduct their own performance evaluations, select new team members, prepare budgets, plan training, schedule vacations, and coordinate work with other teams as well as with management. A number of ways in which self-directed work teams differ from traditional employee involvement are illustrated in Figure 2.

	TRADITIONAL EMPLOYEE INVOLVEMENT	SELF-DIRECTED WORK TEAMS
ROLES:	Fixed	Interchangeable
TASKS:	Rigid	Flexible
SKILLS:	Specialized	Multiskilled
CONTROL:	Individual	Group
STATUS:	Differential	Equal
SUPERVISION:	Outside of group	Within the group
WORK EFFORT:	Divided	Cohesive

Figure 2. How Traditional Employee Involvement and Self-Directed Work Teams Differ

PRINCIPLES GOVERNING SELF-DIRECTED WORK TEAMS

For a self-directed work team to be successful, the following principles are necessary:

1. It must be semiautonomous;

2. It must contain multiple skills; and

3. Its leadership must be shared.

Semiautonomy. Although self-directed work teams report to management, they function in a semiautonomous manner and are responsible for controlling the physical and functional boundaries of their work areas. Within the identified work area, a team can do whatever is necessary to improve all work processes. The team is ultimately responsible for delivering a specified quantity and quality of a product or service within a specified time and at a defined cost.

Multiple skills. Each member of a self-directed work team possesses a variety of skills, unlike employees in traditional organizations who are skilled only in the narrow ranges of their sharply defined positions. Clearly, organizations can benefit from employees who can "wear different hats" and help their peers in a crisis—a deadline, a sudden resignation, and so on. Team members assume the responsibility for training within the work team and provide performance evaluations when applicable.

Shared leadership. Self-directed work teams are not led by a single individual. Rather, team members share and rotate leadership responsibilities equally. Team members have equal input in decisions concerning key issues such as work quality, costs, schedules, safety, and employee-management relations.

PROCESSES SUPPORTING EACH PRINCIPLE

Obviously, one cannot simply mention the above three principles and request that a work team become self-directed. In this section, the processes associated with each principle describe the norms that must be in place before a work team can function in a self-directed, empowered manner (see Figure 3).

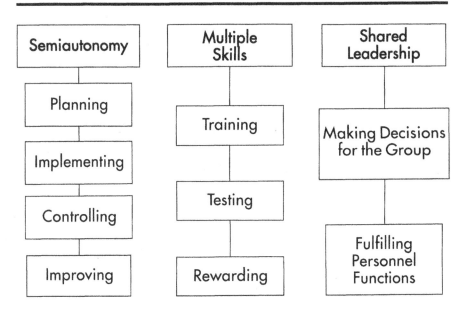

Figure 3. Principles Governing Self-Directed Work Teams and the Processes that Support These Principles

Principle I: Semiautonomous Group Functioning

Semiautonomous behavior is the foundation upon which successful self-directed work teams are built. Self-directed work teams are responsible not only for the tasks themselves but for *planning, implementing, controlling,* and *improving* those tasks. These functions are management's responsibility in more traditional organizations. Of course, self-directed work teams still are accountable to management for work schedules, costs, work quality, and achievement of production goals. Work teams must support, advise, and consult with management and other work teams to maximize production efficiency and overall effectiveness.

Planning. Self-directed work teams have the authority to arrange their own schedules and workflow patterns. They can set work schedules in accordance with organizational guidelines, establish priorities, assign tasks to team members, schedule vacations and other time off, set meeting times, determine materials needed, and adjust tasks and priorities in the event of absenteeism.

Implementing. Self-directed work teams are effective at getting work done. The work-team structure is unique in that all aspects of production are the responsibility of the team members. Members have the power to: (1) implement changes in their work procedures in order to improve the quality of the products or services that they produce; (2) order materials needed to complete their tasks; and (3) perform quality inspections of their products or services.

Controlling. Self-directed work teams are responsible for monitoring themselves and ensuring that their output meets organizational standards of quality. In addition, they must assess the effects of changes in processes upon quality, production rate, and individuals.

Improving. Team members should be trained in all aspects of the quality-improvement process, including statistical-process-control (SPC) methods. The work teams are, of course, accountable to management for production requirements, equipment, technology, and any areas that are fixed by market demand. Because management is responsible for the overall strategic direction of the organization, it maintains the authority to determine all bottom-line costs, quality standards, and production deadlines. However, management is also expected to distribute information, give performance feedback, provide needed training in both technical and human-relations skills, and furnish all essential tools of the trade to work-team members.

The work-team members are responsible as a whole for effective intergroup communication and collaboration in their work efforts, both within their own team and to other work teams (usually through a coordinator or designated team leader) with whom they interact. They ensure that work flows smoothly through the channels as it moves from one group to another. The semiautonomous nature of these work teams empowers team members and allows them to respond as work environments and priorities change, rather than to wait passively for management to come to the rescue. In the process, group identity, team cohesion, and commitment to the team effort grows stronger.

Principle II: Multiskilled Group Functioning

Self-directed work teams function effectively because they are multiskilled; they take on the functions of *training, testing,* and *rewarding.* Although individuals within a team may specialize in different areas, all team members are trained to perform all steps required to complete their group task. Multiskilled workers have the experience and adaptability to respond effectively and efficiently to constant changes in their product or service requirements. Managers of self-directed work teams should bear in mind that continued training and appropriate rewards must be commensurate with the work in order for multiskilled group functioning to be most effective.

Training. Most training and development of a self-directed work team must take place within the team itself, that is, the more highly skilled team members must assume the responsibility for training junior workers. Management is obligated to provide specialized training in areas such as SPC or human-relations skills to help prepare self-directed work teams to function successfully.

Testing. Each member of a self-directed work team must be able to demonstrate adequate proficiency in required skills. Skill levels can be tested by qualified team members through either written exams or on-the-job testing. Acquisition and mastery of work-related skills becomes the responsibility of all team members.

Rewarding. Team members must be recognized and rewarded for skill acquisition and professional development. Recognition can consist of promotion within the team, job reclassification, or public announcement. In addition, "pay for knowledge" based on the idea that "the more you know, the more you are worth" should be another dimension of the reward system.

Principle III: Shared Leadership in Group Functioning

Shared leadership implies that all members of a team work together as a unit, rotating and sharing leadership responsibilities. For example, an organization might decide to elect team leaders on a yearly basis. These people are voted in (and could at any time be voted out), are given leadership responsibilities, and are paid more to compensate for their additional duties. Leaders do not need to exhibit traditional supervisory behaviors such as controlling, planning, and enforcing work activity because self-directed work teams are designed to regulate and govern themselves, making decisions for the group and fulfilling personnel functions.

Leadership in self-directed work teams is functional rather than authoritarian. Leaders are selected because of their knowledge and experience, not because of their job titles. The system of rotational leadership empowers team members, enabling them to make the most of their roles as leaders. Various methods for initiating the rotation are possible.

Making decisions for the group. Self-directed work teams make most of the decisions affecting them and their work. In some organizations, they can hire, fire, determine salary rates (based on skill level), assess quality, establish standard operating procedures, and manage inventory. Therefore, all team members must be adequately trained in technical and human-relations skills such as data collection, problem solving, process improvement, group dynamics, communication skills, and conflict resolution.

Fulfilling personnel functions. Self-directed work teams assume the responsibility for recruiting, selecting, and training new team members; guidelines for these processes are established jointly by management and the team. Work teams are permitted to conduct appraisals of their peers' performances, to reward good performance, and, if necessary, to determine the causes of poor performance so that corrective action can be taken.

POSITIVE ASPECTS OF SELF-DIRECTED WORK TEAMS

Self-directed work teams can have the following positive effects on their organizations:

- Work flow improves;
- Employee-retention rates increase;
- Employee flexibility increases;
- The quality of products and services increases;
- The quantity of products and services may increase;
- Supervisory staff is reduced;
- Performance appraisals are more accurate;
- Salary ranges are established objectively;
- Groups identify and agree on candidates for promotion;
- Equitable, objective, and defensible systems that satisfy equal-employment-opportunity and affirmative-action guidelines are implemented; and

♦ Training, education, and skill deficiencies are easily identified.

As with any change, the implementation of these teams can create a measure of resistance as well as additional start-up costs. Organizations may find themselves coping with the following:

♦ Increased training costs;

♦ Need for additional training staff;

♦ Management's resistance to change;

♦ Lack of enthusiasm by team members in initial meetings; and

♦ Competition between work-team members.

When weighing the pros against the cons, organizations considering the implementation of self-directed work teams should remember that negatives such as increased costs and resistance to change, though practically inevitable with any sweeping change in policies and procedures, are temporary, while the benefits outlined above can be permanent and financially redeeming in the long run. Not all of the processes discussed need be present initially. Selection of the ideal work-team model will vary with differences in type of work, employees' readiness level, and the organizational culture.

Any change agent who works with newly formed work teams also needs to remember that society generally teaches its members to compete against one another and to work independently. At a very young age, children are taught that working together on tests constitutes cheating and that they are rewarded with high grades for excelling over their classmates. However, the

general guidelines outlined in this chapter will
be applicable to any type of work-team model.

CHAPTER SUMMARY

Properly trained and implemented into an organization, a self-directed work team can be
totally responsible for a segment of the organizational process. Self-directed work teams have
the authority to plan, implement, control, and
improve themselves and their work because
management has delegated these responsibilities. Unlike the traditional organizational
setup, in which employees have fixed roles, narrow ranges of tasks, and are supervised and
controlled from the outside, self-directed work
teams are interdependent, flexible, and self
governed. This arrangement is superior to the
traditional employee-manager setup in that employees feel more involved and in control; fewer
levels of management are necessary; and product quality and quantity tend to increase.

REFERENCES

Peters, T. (1987). *Thriving on chaos.* New York:
Harper & Row.

CHAPTER 2

SELECTING THE APPROPRIATE
WORK-TEAM MODEL

*Every business organization is a team—
or team of teams.... Companies and
individuals are players in one or
another game who must defeat their
opponents in a league known as the
marketplace.... Different team sports
have different requirements for team
work and coaching.... These differences
have close parallels in business.
(Keidel, 1985, p. 1)*

Many organizations function without an awareness of the basic work-design models under which they operate. These organizations could be helped to function more efficiently and effectively if they were made aware of the different types of work-team models and if they were shown which models were most suited to their work styles and objectives. In manufacturing and service organizations, for example, the most influential factor in determining the configuration of a self-directed work team will be the tasks themselves. To be most effective, the form that a work team takes must follow the functions that the team is expected to carry out. The use of models, especially general ones with which most people are familiar, also can illustrate the strengths and weaknesses of various organizational designs.

Some managers believe that self-directed work teams can be successfully implemented only in cultures that value cooperation and collaboration (for example, in Scandinavia and Japan). They fear that their organizations would have difficulty establishing self-directed work teams because of the individualistic and competitive nature of their Western cultures. However, many cultures—even those that stress competition, not collaboration, in the work place—value the concept of the team in athletic pursuits. Most people have at some time been involved with athletic teams, either as players, coaches, rule keepers, or spectators. These roles, and several popular sports, provide some basic models of team functioning that lend themselves to application in an organizational setting. The primary sports that will be discussed are baseball, football, and basketball. Volleyball and tennis are organized variations of the previous three sports and will be examined later in the chapter.

A SPORTS SYNOPSIS

The following descriptions contain the elements of the sports that relate to work teams:

Baseball. Baseball is a highly individualistic sport that occasionally requires teamwork in certain circumstances. Players interact minimally, and coordination of players is achieved through the design of the game.

Football. The game of football demands organized, systematic teamwork. Plays are designed in advance, and players are assigned specialized roles throughout the game and for each play. Careful planning ensures player cooperation and collaboration.

Basketball. Basketball players are required to achieve spontaneous teamwork. Coordination is achieved as the players mutually and simultaneously adjust to the changing circumstances of the game. Basketball is a fast-moving game requiring great flexibility and harmony among its players.

Volleyball. Volleyball, similar to basketball, is a sport that requires spontaneous action as a team. The players, who operate within semifixed positions, are not permitted the free movement allowed members of a basketball team. Volleyball players achieve coordination through mutual adjustments within a fixed zone of play.

Tennis. Tennis, a highly individualistic sport, requires each player to perform either alone or in partnership (as in doubles) to win. A tennis team is a group of players that has common coaching (supervision), plays for a cumulative score (product or service), and has group identification.

ATHLETIC TEAMS AS WORK-TEAM MODELS

The Baseball-Team Model

The individual is the basic unit in baseball. Player interaction is minimal, and usually only two or three players on the same team are involved in any one play. Team success (scoring) is determined by totaling each team member's individual performance (points earned), and team coordination is produced by the design of the work itself.

Examining the roles of baseball-team members, one notices that not all players can play every position. The pitcher and catcher, for example, are trained in highly specialized positions, whereas other team members may be rotated in and out of various positions. For example, outfielders may prefer a specific field, but they are capable of playing any outfield position. Infielders, on the other hand, have more specialized roles and are less apt to exchange positions. However, infielders support one another when the ball is in play, for example, in a closely integrated and swiftly executed double play.

Some organizations are set up much like baseball teams; a good example is an insurance com-

On a baseball team, players are highly individualistic;
coordination is achieved through the design of the game.

pany. This service-oriented organization has a sales force made up of high-performing individuals who require little direction and interaction. The salesperson, like the pitcher on a baseball team, initiates the action by contacting prospective clients. Like a batter, a salesperson may step up to the plate many times before hitting a home run; like a pitcher, a salesperson has to throw many balls before striking a player out.

Other members of the insurance team, such as underwriters, claims adjusters, and clerical personnel, are similar to infielders and outfielders in that they support the play as needed. They function in an integrated manner to satisfy team-member and customer needs.

In a production-oriented organization, such as a construction company or a shipyard, specialized tradespeople such as welders, carpenters, electricians, and plumbers must function together like a baseball team in order to achieve their objectives. The layout person, like a pitcher, initiates all construction activity. Other workers function more like infielders and outfielders; they work in specialized areas but must be prepared to function in different capacities and to work together when circumstances require.

Effective baseball-type work teams have a number of common characteristics:

1. *Autonomy.* Each team member works relatively independently.

2. *Initiative.* Team members are expected to exercise their knowledge and influence in their areas of expertise.

3. *Flexibility.* Members must be able to carry out a variety of independent tasks, the order and priorities of which can change unpredictably.

4. *Contribution.* All tasks performed by team members culminate in an end product.

5. *Infrequent Interaction.* Any interactions between members are brief and infrequent. Team members do not work in close collaboration.

The key to success with the baseball-team model is the effective management of task interdependence; in other words, the process of integrating the parts together to compose a whole. This type of work team relies on *pooled independence.* In this model, the parts are relatively independent of each other but make contributions to the organizational effort. Pooled independence implies that the individuals are soloists or independent players like those on a baseball team.

Service- and production-oriented organizations may benefit from the application of the baseball-team model. Employees in these types of organizations are often overspecialized and poorly integrated as teams. They often compete fiercely with one another, which may interfere with the achievement of the larger goals of their organizations. The average shipyard crew, for example, may contain workers in seven different trades, each with its own budget, blueprints, and deadlines. This same group of employees might belong to five different unions, each with its own set of procedures and standards.

Such organizations may increase productivity by helping employees agree on a common purpose, by facilitating improved communication among team members, by promoting a sense of group cohesion, and by introducing problem-solving techniques. As communication and collaboration replace competition, systems tend to flow more smoothly, paving the way for increased productivity.

The Football-Team Model

Although actions by individuals are important in football, this game demands greater team interaction than does baseball. In the game of football, every player on the field participates actively in every play. Success (scoring) is determined by the team's ability to perform as a unit. A good football team consists of a defense that acts as a wall through which the opposing team cannot penetrate and an aggressive offense that finds the other team's weak spots and takes advantage of them. Team coordination is achieved under the planning and direction of coaches and specialists who also must function as a unified force to communicate their messages.

A self-directed work team based on the football-team model consists of individuals who occupy distinct positions; the ordering and hierarchy of these positions are determined by the skills needed to accomplish the team's task. Key positions on the team are awarded to individuals who have mastered specialized technical skills. These key "players" are supported by individuals whose jobs are less technically complex and more interchangeable.

On a football team, the quarterback holds the most important position. The quarterback deter-

On a football team, players are assigned specialized roles;
careful planning ensures their cooperation and collaboration.

mines each play's strategy, calls signals, and handles the ball on every play. The group of players that is next highest in importance (backfield runners, pass receivers, and blockers) have varying levels of significance; a player may be critical in one play and less so in another. Although the contribution of the left tackle or guard is always critical to the success of the play, that person never carries the ball.

This work-team model can be compared to service-oriented organizations, such as hospitals. In a hospital setting, the doctor, like the quarterback, makes a diagnosis and determines the "play" or course of action. Nurses and anesthesiologists, like the backfield, have somewhat less critical roles (based on their skills), while the rest of the team fulfills the support function.

In a highly technical, production-oriented operation such as an engineering company, the most prominent person is usually the chief engineer or the production designer. Like a quarterback, this person would be instrumental in formulating strategy and in initiating action. A production designer is supported by highly trained technicians and supporting team members who work with him or her to achieve the team's objective. Success in a football-model work team hinges on the planning and direction of trained technical experts who coordinate a complex set of sequential activities.

Effective football-type work teams have a number of common characteristics:

1. *Effective Planning.* Execution of individual tasks is coordinated through a comprehensive, prerehearsed plan of action.

2. *Efficient Coordination of Complex Parts.* Success can be achieved only if all members' actions are carefully coordinated.

3. *Predetermined Sequence of Action.* Tasks must be carried out in a controlled order.

4. *Equal Contribution Among Members.* All team members must pull their own weight.

5. *Constant Communication.* Members must interact frequently and must tailor their communication styles to suit the task at hand.

The key to success when implementing the football-team model is the effective management of specialized tasks. A work group patterned after a football team stresses controlled and sequential interdependence. Each team member relies heavily on the cooperation of others in order to complete tasks successfully. One might think of the model of sequential interdependence as an orchestra of individual members who must follow a predetermined plan and are led by a conductor.

Organizations suited to the adoption of the football-team model often place highly skilled technicians and professionals in roles of authority that are outside the scope of their training. Often, these specialists are neither interested nor skilled in performing management functions. It is important for organizations to recognize that this may not be the most efficient method of utilizing these resources.

Self-directed work teams modeled after football teams can become more efficient by allowing the highly skilled technicians on the team to function like quarterbacks. The quarterback calls the plays but is not responsible for general team management. Rather, the management function is shared by all team members, thus allowing the quarterback to concentrate solely on his task.

The Basketball-Team Model

The self-directed work-team model that requires the most interaction is based on the basketball team, in which players interact with their teammates in a highly flexible manner. Players frequently swap roles and positions as circumstances change. Each player is trained to fill all positions and can assume any role during the game. Success is dependent on the team's ability to perform as a continuous, interdependent unit; coordination is achieved through the players' ability to function as a unit without extensive planning or direction.

Although basketball players begin with a plan of action, they have the freedom to react spontaneously to the changing nature of the game. Players are assigned to positions such as center, guard, and forward, and all are trained in fundamental skills such as shooting, passing, and dribbling the ball. Basketball spectators may notice players' freedom on the court because they have difficulty distinguishing one player's position from another. Because team members are so interdependent, practically all players can be credited with helping with each score.

Examples of organizations that fit the basketball-team model include the creative advertising agency, the think tank, or the ad hoc task force. In this type of team, a highly skilled group of professionals engage in creative efforts. In the

On a basketball team, players are required to achieve spontaneous teamwork, necessitating great flexibility and harmony.

way that a basketball team passes the ball around until it scores, this type of work team passes ideas around until it hits upon a successful idea. Each team member has equal responsibility for generating ideas and for supporting other team members. All members have equal status, and they are limited only by the extent of their knowledge, skills, and creativity.

In production organizations such as steel mills and automotive plants, highly integrated teams of skilled workers function as interdependent units to fulfill task assignments. For example, in a team-oriented automotive-production plant like Volvo, cars are completely assembled by teams of six to eight workers. All team members are expected to learn and execute all skills needed to assemble a car. Due to scheduling, material delays, or absenteeism, group members must be able to shift and adjust to changing work conditions.

Effective basketball-type work teams have a number of common characteristics:

1. *Spontaneity.* Team members must be flexible and able to assume one another's duties at any time.

2. *Cooperation.* Team members must work together smoothly; one person's actions must complement another's.

3. *Equal and Enthusiastic Participation.* Every member participates actively and takes the initiative when he or she feels it necessary.

4. *Effective Communication and Interaction.* Members interact constantly in a wide variety of ways and can adapt to changing circumstances.

The key to success with the basketball-team model is the effective management of task integration. This type of work team relies on reciprocal interdependence, which means that every member of the team interacts with every other member. In this model, success depends more on interaction among team members than on the outstanding achievements of any one player. A musical analogy of this type of work team would be a jazz band, whose members generally follow the music but adapt to one another's improvisations, thus creating an original piece with each performance.

Organizations suited to the basketball-team model often are organized in ways that do not effectively utilize employees' skills. Employees sometimes are placed in highly supervised production systems in which cooperation, adaptability, and creativity are seldom allowed. These types of organizations can become more effective by teaching individuals about empowerment and encouraging them to work together to increase job satisfaction and job productivity.

Variation I: The Volleyball-Team Model

Like a basketball team, a volleyball team consists of individuals who must be able to perform all of the team's tasks. The main difference between the two is in the level of technical skill required to do the job.

A volleyball team is made up of individuals who have mastered the moderately technical tasks required to accomplish a specific goal. This type of work team rotates tasks and positions on a regular basis. All team members take turns

On a volleyball team, players achieve coordination
through mutual adjustments within a fixed zone of play.

leading, coordinating, and performing. The leader serves, the spiker performs, and the set-up person assists; all players work together in a coordinated manner to achieve their objective.

Like a volleyball team, an assembly-and-production unit trains its team members to perform all related tasks to ensure a high degree of flexibility in the production cycle. Team members coordinate their functions, support one another, share responsibilities, and make joint decisions that impact the entire team. In fast-food operations, for example, team members receive ongoing training on all work stations. Many operations employ a trainer or coach to supervise the training process.

This type of organization is prone to a high turnover rate because it typically pays poorly and does not foster strong employee loyalty. Therefore, there is an opportunity for such organizations to benefit greatly from the implementation of self-directed work teams. Group identity and employee empowerment can help to cut turnover; morale and productivity can also increase because team members direct and control their own work. Like a good volleyball team, members of this type of self-directed work team identify with the team, function cooperatively, and inspire the motivation needed to succeed.

Variation II: The Tennis-Team Model

Another kind of self-directed work team is made up of individuals whose work styles would not appear at first to be suited to a work-team model. These individuals usually work alone and rarely have the need to work in teams. Like

On a tennis team, players have common coaching, play
for a cumulative score, and have group identification.

the members of a tennis team, each person works separately with a customer or project but is still considered a member of the team. The common traits that characterize a tennis team are common leadership, shared communication, group support, and cumulative scores.

An example of an organization that fits the tennis-team model is a sales force consisting of individuals who interact with customers one-on-one and whose cumulative efforts spell success or failure for the organization. When forming this type of work team, a manager or consultant should stress the sharing of a vision, adequate training, product and customer information, individual and team recognition, and rewards. Most organizations do not fit the tennis-team model, because they require close cooperation among employees. However, specific parts of organizations may fit the model. For example, a group of research scientists could work together to develop a cure for a disease but would work independently to solve problems as they arose.

In work environments in which the tennis-team model is appropriate, employees work on separate tasks that contribute to the successful completion of the team's task. Implementation of the tennis-team model can help to increase job commitment and employee satisfaction by fostering greater cooperation and intragroup support.

Using the sports-team analogy as an analytical tool, organizations can select the most appropriate work-team model that suits its particular needs. To sum up the three main models, the baseball team emphasizes autonomy; the football team control; and the basketball team cooperation. Each model has its own strengths and weaknesses.

THE MANAGER AS COACH

Managers of self-directed work teams play a critical and active role. These managers are more like athletic-team coaches than traditional managers. Traditional managers control most aspects of the work and allow employees little input in decisions that concern them and their work. Athletic-team coaches, on the other hand, relinquish control of team members' actions once the team is on the field. A coach's position is literally and figuratively on the sidelines. Managers of self-directed work teams, like athletic coaches, strive to coordinate their team members' actions to foster productivity and success. The techniques that they employ vary with the type of work-team model with which they are working.

Managers of baseball-type work teams rely on their ability to effectively select and deploy individual players and to weave them together into a cohesive unit. Close monitoring and supervising of this type of team tends to be counterproductive, because players need the freedom to exercise their unique work styles.

Managers of football-type work teams must be able to plan and coordinate a complex system of production or service efforts. They must be superior organizers, planners, and trainers. They must be able to mesh the contributions of a diverse group of specialists into a composite product. The manager of a football-type work team is responsible for preparing a comprehensive plan of action, rehearsing it with the team, and motivating the team to perform in an empowered manner.

Managers of basketball-type work teams must be excellent facilitators. They must develop the work team's ability to self-coordinate. Because a basketball-type work team works with a flow of activities that cannot be predicted, the manager must concentrate on developing a team that can adjust to a rapidly changing environment. The manager must be able to influence, motivate, and critique team members' work; in other words, the manager must be skilled in the management of interdependence. Successful "coaching" depends on the manager's direction and the team's ability to act outside that direction when needed.

Effective managers of self-directed work teams have in common several skills:

1. *Leadership Skills.* Managers must be able to communicate the organization's vision, mission, and values to team members, including values concerning standards, production rates, and schedules.

2. *Communication and Facilitation Skills.* Managers must have the skills needed to facilitate communication among members, teams, and the organization as a whole.

3. *Training Skills.* Managers must ensure that all team members receive any needed training in technical and human-relations skills.

4. *Consulting Skills.* Managers must be able to help teams solve both technical and interpersonal problems; they also must have enough experience to realize that a problem is beyond

their scope of training and that it must be referred elsewhere.

5. *Problem-Solving Skills.* The manager must be able to act as a troubleshooter to steer the team clear of problems that the members may not be able to predict or recognize.

6. *Feedback Skills.* The manager must be able to provide performance feedback to teams and team members and to recognize and reward success.

Clearly, the manager's role is critical to the successful establishment of a self-directed work-team system. Managers must assume a role that emphasizes facilitation skills rather than control skills. Even though fewer managers are required to supervise self-directed work teams, they are key to organizational transformation.

TOP MANAGEMENT AS GAMEKEEPERS

Every sport has officials who enforce the rules of the game, for example, umpires and referees; their job is to make sure that the rules (a common set of agreed-on standards) are observed. The referees of an organization are the employees who comprise top management. Their role is to determine the overall strategic direction of the organization; they decide the nature of their company's game. Top management observes the workings of their organization, only becoming involved with systems and processes if the organization's standards are violated.

CHAPTER SUMMARY

Society has within it an appropriate model—the athletic team—for understanding and establishing self-directed work teams. When the analogy of the athletic team is used, work-team styles appropriate to specific types of organizations can be identified, understood, and maximized. By understanding the models presented in this chapter, management can more effectively carry out their responsibility in methods appropriate to the particular work team. Organizations will benefit from studying the athletic-team model and applying it internally.

REFERENCES

Keidel, R. (1985). *Game plans*. New York: E.P. Dutton.

CHAPTER 3

HOW SELF-DIRECTED WORK TEAMS CAN BENEFIT ORGANIZATIONS

A single person using quality improvement practices can make a difference. But rarely does a single person have enough knowledge or experience to understand everything that goes on in a process. Therefore, major gains in quality and productivity most often result from teams—a group of people, their skills, talents, and knowledge. With proper training, teams can tackle complex and chronic problems and come up with effective, permanent solutions. (Scholtes, 1988, p. 2-7)

Organizations that implement the self-directed work-team approach can expect gains in efficiency and, therefore, a positive impact on the organizational bottom line. This chapter will explain and illustrate the benefits that self-directed work teams can produce. These benefits can take the form of (1) increased productivity, (2) improved service and product quality, (3) increased employee morale, and (4) reduced overhead. Figure 4 below illustrates the relationship between these benefits.

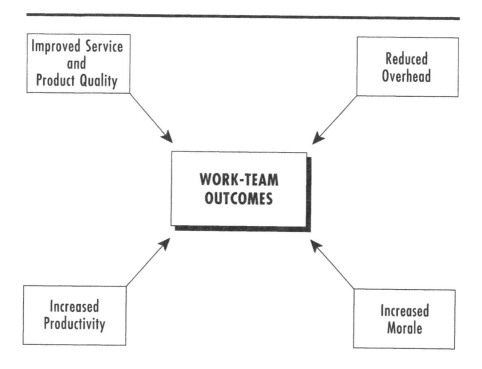

Figure 4. How Self-Directed Work Teams
Can Benefit Organizations

INCREASED PRODUCTIVITY

Increased productivity can be defined as the ability to furnish results, benefits, or profits in abundance. Self-directed work teams can increase their productivity by improving work methods and procedures, which in turn allows them to improve efficiency, rate of output, product and service quality, thereby cutting waste and reducing the need to redo completed tasks.

If immediate communication is allowed within the work group, the decision-making process can be improved and time can be saved. Because self-directed work teams often have lower rates of absenteeism and tardiness and can implement measures to improve safety on the job, they can help to produce a work ethic of regular, prompt attendance, a high level of effort on the job, and a high degree of safety, all of which contribute to high productivity.

The earliest demonstrations of productivity increases related to work-team efforts were first documented by Britain's Tavistock Institute during an investigation of the relationship between technology, work design, and productivity in coal mines. The researchers at the Tavistock Institute found that productivity increased when work teams were established to integrate technological changes with the human factors. They discovered that teams made better decisions with regard to scheduling, job sequencing, job assignments, production methods, determining team membership, and compensation (Lawler, 1986).

In the early 1950s, General Foods experimented with the use of self-directed work teams in a newly opened plant in Topeka, Kansas. The experiment proved successful: unit costs dropped to 5 percent less than those in similar factories— a savings of $1 million. Employee turnover was only 8 percent, and the first accident causing a worker to lose time occurred almost four years after the plant opened. Although the experiment was successful, it was not regarded favorably by traditionally structured organizations and was eventually discontinued (Lawler, 1986).

In the 1970s, the autonomous work-team design was tested by the Swedish automotive industry. Suffering from high employee turnover (45 to 70 percent per year) and a 20-percent absenteeism rate, the Saab and Volvo automotive manufacturers established work assembly teams. These teams were allowed to plan, schedule, and establish their own work paces (Hunsaker & Curtis, 1986). Over a ten-year period, the Swedish Volvo-Kalmar plant experienced the following changes attributable to the work teams' efforts:

- Total time spent on each car produced dropped by 40 percent;
- Inventory turnover increased from nine times a year to twenty-one times a year; and
- Production output increased from 96 to 99 percent.

Volvo-Kalmar now has the lowest assembly costs of all Volvo plants. The plant also shows the lowest figure of office-employee person-hours per car produced (Aguren, 1985). Other similar success stories exist. Workers at a General Electric plant achieved production schedules 50 percent faster than management's estimate after redesigning their jobs (Sherwood,

1988). A packaging team at the Proctor & Gamble's soap plant in Ohio redesigned, installed, and implemented an innovation in packaging that was based on one team member's idea (Sherwood, 1988). The Gaines Pet Food plant in Topeka, Kansas, has reduced the unit cost of its products almost every year for the fifteen years since it initiated work teams (Hunsaker & Curtis, 1986). Westinghouse Canada's redesigned manufacturing facility at Airdire, Alberta, reduced cycle time for made-to-order motor-control devices from more than seventeen weeks to one produced every week (Hunsaker & Curtis, 1986).

INCREASED QUALITY

High and consistent quality can be defined as the degree to which a product or service meets the customer's requirements and specifications. Self-directed work teams can increase the quality of products and services because their members are able to implement quality-control improvements and to use a method—known as *statistical process control*—of resolving issues concerning quality. They can also increase quality because they have greater authority and control over the work process, thereby increasing individual accountability for production quality. Work-team members can identify with and feel pride in the production of a product or service with which they are involved. According to Cummings and Molloy (1977), six out of seven studies of self-directed work teams reported improvements in quality.

The aforementioned Volvo-Kalmar plant emphasized the value of quality ("doing the job right") to its workers. The workers responded positively to personalized, timely feedback. Workers' satisfaction with their production of quality products motivated them to strive for a zero-error rate. Over the ten-year period of study, the defect rate dropped by 39 percent (Aguren, 1985).

Service organizations also can boost quality with the use of self-directed work teams; this accomplishment is generally based on the realization that the work team (the front-line employees who have direct customer contact) are the people who know the most about their customers' needs and wants. In Japan, this technique has been applied successfully by organizations such as Hotel Okura, Yaesu Book Center, and Mk Taxi as part of total-quality-control programs. Employee groups have helped to reorganize systems in order to increase consumers' comfort, to decrease waiting time, and to encourage employees' helpful attitude toward customers. They have achieved this by encouraging teams to explore the causes of poor service and to take corrective action (Gardner, 1989).

There are a number of service-focused work teams in the United States. Organizations such as Inter-First Bank, General Dynamics Corporation, Standard Meat Company, and Miller Brewing Company work to improve service quality with the use of service-focused work teams. After self-directed work teams were introduced into the policyholder service area at Shenandoah Life Insurance Company, the employee-to-supervisor ratio changed from 7:1 to 15:1, service improved, and complaints and errors declined (Sherwood, 1988).

Ford's automotive-assembly plant in Hermo-sillo, Mexico, has only one job classification for all assembly workers, who are responsible for all quality control and on-line maintenance. When necessary, workers can stop the assembly line. During their first year, this plant established a lower defect rate than that of most Japanese automobile makers (Sherwood, 1988).

At Aetna Life's benefits claim office in Rocky Hill, Connecticut, each twelve-person team han-dles the various claims-handling functions that once were divided among several departments. They also manage their own work flow, schedul-ing, overtime, hiring, and performance evalua-tions (Sherwood, 1988).

Xerox chairman David Kearns learned a lesson from his adversaries and in 1983 launched an all-out campaign for quality. Appealing to the firm's 100,000 workers, Xerox formed employee teams to encourage shop-floor innovation and cooperative problem solving (Gardner, 1989).

Milliken, a family-owned manufacturer of prod-ucts ranging from computer tape to carpets and tennis-ball covers, launched a quality campaign that required a top-to-bottom restructuring of the company's operations. Milliken set strict new production standards and formed employee teams to work with customers and suppliers to tailor the manufacturing process more closely to buyers' needs (Keidel, 1985).

During the four years following the opening of Honeywell's circuit board plant in Chandler, Arizona, the quality yield increased from 82 percent to 99.5 percent. At the same time, waste decreased from 18 percent to 1.5 percent, unit costs were reduced to 46 percent of their original levels, and output increased by 280 percent (Sherwood, 1988).

The quality yield at Zilog's wafer-fabrication plant in Nampa, Idaho, has been 90 to 95 percent since its start-up in 1978, compared with an average industry yield of 75 percent (Sherwood, 1988).

INCREASED EMPLOYEE MORALE

Employee morale can be defined as the positive emotional condition (enthusiasm, confidence, loyalty, and so on) of a person or group with regard to that person's or group's tasks on the job. Self-directed work teams can help to create satisfying and rewarding work environments, thereby producing positive employee attitudes, increasing productivity, and reducing costs.

Membership in work teams helps to satisfy people's needs to belong, to interact with others, to receive recognition, and to achieve. When organizations offer pay raises for the acquisition of multiple skills and bonuses based on achievement, members of self-directed work teams express even higher levels of satisfaction. Praise from team members also can be a strong source of motivation; conversely, team members know that they can be terminated for poor performance. These factors probably contribute to the lower number of days that work-team members are off sick. Finally, because work teams produce more satisfied employees, the result is greater retention with less employee turnover.

NASCO, an American shipbuilding company, experimented with work teams in 1985 and discovered that this method of organizing labor could benefit the organization. Although not all goals were fully realized, most team members reported that their time on the work team was a positive experience. Furthermore, team members indicated that working as a team helped to increase their motivation, skill levels, and morale ("Multi-Skilled," 1987).

The Kalmar-Volvo plant experienced a significant decrease in employee turnover and absenteeism over a ten-year period when work teams were initiated. Most of the employees who participated believed that the work-team structure was positive. They believed that their jobs on the work team were better than the jobs of typical assembly-line workers. The study results indicated an increasingly positive atmosphere in the plant. Employees became more interested in learning more about production and about the general operation of the plant (Keidel, 1985).

At a General Foods plant in Iowa, the corporate business-team manager visits the plant and briefs each new team of employees on the company's product, market, competition, and business plan (Keidel, 1985). For more than fifteen years, the Gaines Pet Food plant in Topeka, Kansas, has had an open storeroom, and employees have keys to the main door of the plant, a privilege that clearly indicates the high level of trust between employees and management (Huse & Cummings, 1985).

Turnover at Zilog's wafer fabrication plant in Idaho has been as low as 2 to 6 percent, compared with an average of 50 to 55 percent for workers producing integrated circuit chips in California's Silicon Valley during the same time period (Sherwood, 1988).

REDUCED OVERHEAD

Overhead can be defined as any business expense, such as rent, insurance, or supervision, that is not chargeable to a particular sector of the production process. Obviously, reduction of overhead costs results in an increased bottom line.

In organizations using work teams, many tasks traditionally assigned to supervisory staff can be assigned directly to work teams, thereby effecting a significant reduction in overhead. Significant gains in productivity can then be achieved by hiring fewer supervisors and support personnel.

Plants with established work teams usually can lower their total production costs by an estimated 20 to 40 percent (Lawler, 1986). For example, in General Motors' plant in Livonia, Michigan, the implementation of self-directed work teams eliminated the middle-management level, and the number of foremen was reduced by 40 percent; those remaining were retitled *team coordinators* (Peters, 1987).

The Sharonville, Ohio, Ford plant eliminated its general-supervisor level. In its place, a zone superintendent and an assistant were hired to plan, coordinate, and solve problems (Peters, 1987).

By 1987, several of the most advanced Ford and General Motors plants, which employ up to one thousand people, had removed all forms of supervisory roles except for a solitary plant manager (Peters, 1987).

At the Johnsonville Sausage Company, all forms of formal supervision (including that of plant manager) have been eliminated from its four plants. Teams known as "Pride Teams" manage the entire operation (Peters, 1987).

Over a four-year period at the Dana Corporation, the corporate staff was reduced from nearly 475 to less than 100, and the number of management levels was reduced from about fourteen to six. During this time, sales increased fourfold (Sherwood, 1988).

A paper-products plant in Mehoopany, Pennsylvania, operates with overhead costs that are as much as 35 percent less than those at its conventionally structured sister plant in Green Bay, Wisconsin. The manager-to-employee ratios at the two plants are 1:15 and 1:7, respectively (Sherwood, 1988).

Before the 1983 reorganization of the policyholder service unit at Shenandoah Life, a form was required to pass through the hands of thirty-two people and across nine sections and three departments of the company. This process took twenty-seven days. With the introduction of self-directed clerical teams, supervision was reduced by 80 percent, and the same work was done by one group of six people. These six people also handle 13 percent more paperwork with fewer complaints and errors.

As shown by these examples, many organizations have reduced overhead costs by eliminating and restructuring management positions. In redesigned positions, managers function as consultants rather than as bosses, sometimes increasing their spans of control tenfold.

CHAPTER SUMMARY

Although there is no one path to achieving high production, high quality, reduced overhead, and high morale, the work-team system approach for the organization of labor has demonstrated consistent success in all of these areas. Today's competitive market demands a high level of performance from all employees. Simply complying with rules and obeying supervisors is no longer enough; organizations need employees who are highly committed. Implementation of self-directed work teams increases the probability that organizations will achieve their goals.

REFERENCES

Aguren, S. (1985). *Volvo-Kalmar revisited.* Gottenberg, Sweden: Development Council SAF LO PTC.

Cummings, T.G., & Molloy, E. (1977). *Improving productivity and the quality of work life.* New York: Praeger.

Gardner, H. (1989, November). Time essay. *Time,* pp. 3-7.

Hunsaker, P.L., & Curtis, W. (1986). *Managing organizational behavior.* Reading, MA: Addison-Wesley.

Huse, E.F., & Cummings, T. (1985). *Organization development and change.* St. Paul, MN: West.

Keidel, R. (1985). *Game plans*. New York: E.P. Dutton.

Lawler, E.E. (1986). *High involvement management*. San Francisco: Jossey-Bass.

Multi-skilled, self-managing work teams in a zone-construction environment. (1987, August). Washington, DC: Department of Transportation.

Peters, T. (1987). *Thriving on chaos*. New York: Harper & Row.

Scholtes, P.R. (1988). *The team handbook*. Madison, WI: Joiner Associates.

Sherwood, J.J. (1988, Winter). Creating work cultures with competitive advantage. *Organizational Dynamics*, pp. 5-27.

CHAPTER 4

IMPLEMENTING SELF-DIRECTED WORK TEAMS

ACTION PLAN

Although there is clearly no one path for establishing a high performance, high commitment work team system, the conception, design, implementation, and day-to-day management of this kind of work system requires consistent and continuous attention.
(Sherwood, 1988, p. 5)

The method by which self-directed work teams are implemented in organizations is critical to their success. Because the potential exists for large shifts in organizational structure and changes in the power relationship between employees and management, the work-team concept must be implemented with the active participation of all key people in the organization. Failure to attend to this important dynamic can greatly decrease the program's chances for success. It is difficult to mandate a work-team system by management decree because the very nature of the program relies highly on employee involvement and trust and on management commitment.

The establishment of work-team systems requires a new way of looking at the organization and at how the work is to be accomplished. It requires management to re-evaluate its theories and its role in the change process. Based on differences in organizational systems, the ways that self-directed work teams are implemented will vary.

To effect lasting organizational change, all employees affected by the change(s) must be committed to the implementation of self-directed work teams. If attitudes, values, and beliefs are not changed, and if the political aspects (major constituencies and key individuals) are not managed properly, changes may be short-lived and people may return to "business as usual." This chapter presents a model of three key strategies and three action steps essential for successfully implementing self-directed work-team systems.

Strategy 1: Empower the Work Force

Empowerment is the process of bestowing authority upon a person or group in order to achieve a goal. The degree to which employees feel empowered is critical to the success or failure of the self-directed work team. Giving employees more control over their work increases the probability that they will be more effective at functioning in work-team systems.

The concept of employee participation is not new, and "empowerment" can be confused with employee-participation programs. Organizations have had employee-participation programs, ranging from suggestion boxes to task forces, for the last fifty years. However, the concept of self-directed work teams requires a level of employee involvement seldom seen in the traditional work place.

Most managers are familiar with the information-exchange form of employee participation: managers collect data through surveys, establish suggestion programs, publish newsletters, and give speeches in order to acquire and disseminate information. Decisions based on this information—and often the information itself—remain in the hands of management. A somewhat more empowering form of employee participation is based on group problem solving. Quality Circles and quality-of-work-life programs are good examples of group problem solving. In these programs, employees have greater access to information and are charged with recommending solutions to management. However, the final decision and implementation of the recommendations still are controlled by management.

In an empowering environment, employees have access to all relevant information and are expected to share in the decision-making process with management. Empowerment is the key to self-managed change and a basic tenet for successful work teams. Self-managed change requires employees to actively share their ideas about what is wrong with the system and to suggest changes that should be made to improve work processes. As a result, employees feel more informed, better able to make decisions, and more critical to the success of the organization.

Strategy 2: Develop a Common Language

It is important for an organization to establish a common language—a systematic method for communicating ideas and feelings throughout the organization. This common language can be a learned language such as statistical process control (SPC), or it can be developed by the organization in the form of mission statements, which are operating principles or values that guide the organization. It must, however, be shared and agreed on by everyone in the organization.

In work-team systems, management and employees must often discuss issues related to quality, productivity, and employee morale in an objective manner. The development of a precise common language facilitates the flow of communication, thereby increasing the organization's efficiency. Organizations often turn to their training and development departments to develop communication standards. Such organizations realize that investing in the substantial amount of time and resources required to mount such a comprehensive and continuous training program will pay off with the achievement of organizational goals.

Strategy 3: Maintain a Supportive Culture

A supportive culture is one in which the organizational beliefs, behaviors, interactions, and rules promote the development and maintenance of self-directed work teams. Top management plays the leading role in establishing a supportive culture. Through strategic-planning efforts and the identification of priorities and goals, management must allocate the necessary personnel and resources and be committed and involved in the transformation of their organization. Management must also deal with unions and the "good old boy" network, both powerful stakeholders who often resist the establishment of a work-team culture. Failure to do so will hinder the development of a supportive culture.

Unions have legitimate concerns about issues such as job security, changes in operating procedures, and rewards. However, programs such as gain sharing, team incentive pay, and pay for knowledge can replace traditional programs. Top management must involve union leaders very early in the change process to negotiate a contract that supports the culture of the self-directed work team.

Three Action Steps for Establishing Work-Team Systems

Step 1: Education and Commitment

The first step in developing a work-team program is to educate top management and key stakeholders, who must thoroughly understand the concepts, benefits, and challenges involved in the implementation of work teams. A self-directed work-team system requires many changes in the organizational culture, such as structure, methods of supervision, work design, and rewards.

Top management must be thoroughly familiarized with the concepts of self-directed work teams by reading, by attending conferences and workshops, by seeking expert consultation, and by observing successful work teams. They must be fully committed to taking the necessary steps to support the implementation of the work-team program. Without top management's support and involvement, a successful program will be difficult to achieve.

Likewise, key stakeholders such as workers, union representatives, and supervisors selected for the self-directed work-team pilot program must also read, attend in-house seminars, and take part in discussion groups. They must be fully committed to working as a group to support the implementation of the work-team program. Without key stakeholder support, a successful program is unlikely.

Top management can easily be overwhelmed by the time and expense involved in the implementation of a work-team system. Key stakeholders can feel threatened by proposed changes in the status quo; they may fear a loss of job security, rewards, power, and prestige. Furthermore, all people tend to initially react negatively to the prospect of change because the current situation is routine and familiar, even though it may be less than idyllic. Figure 5 illustrates some common barriers to winning the acceptance of top management and key stakeholders along with alternative strategies for breaking down resistance and gaining support and trust.

Step 2: Planning

Representatives of key stakeholder groups are selected by top management to form a task force whose purpose is to plan, implement, and evaluate a work-team pilot project. This task force must address such issues as communication, problem solving, rewards and punishments, production goals, performance evaluation, scheduling, allocation of task assignments, and the design of the work itself.

Task-Force Formation. During this initial phase, top management must designate key stakeholders who will be in charge of developing methods for implementing the self-directed work team. The task-force members must consider redesigning the work system—including individual tasks, team tasks, and support systems to produce maximum empowerment and technical efficiency. The task force must combine a variety of positions to form an atmosphere in which a team can best complete a product or service.

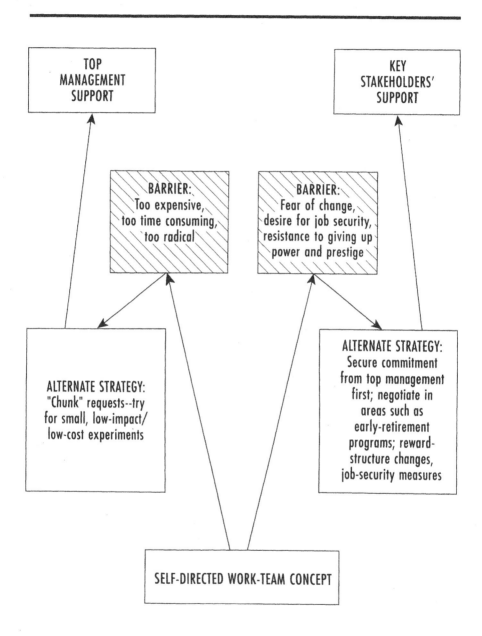

TOP
MANAGEMENT
SUPPORT

KEY
STAKEHOLDERS'
SUPPORT

BARRIER:
Too expensive,
too time consuming,
too radical

BARRIER:
Fear of change,
desire for job security,
resistance to giving up
power and prestige

ALTERNATE STRATEGY:
"Chunk" requests--try
for small, low-impact/
low-cost experiments

ALTERNATE STRATEGY:
Secure commitment
from top management
first; negotiate in
areas such as
early-retirement
programs; reward-
structure changes,
job-security measures

SELF-DIRECTED WORK-TEAM CONCEPT

Figure 5. The Path to Support for the Work-Team Concept

The formation of a task force will be hampered if any of the following is present: (1) inability to acquire proper training, (2) ineffective leadership, or (3) less than full participation. These barriers can be overcome if (1) task-force members are given adequate training in data-collection skills, problem solving, and group decision making; (2) members are provided with adequate expert help in the areas of data collection and data analysis; and (3) top management allows the task force to make decisions within defined boundaries.

Organization Survey. Before beginning any sort of work-team implementation process, it is important to conduct an organization survey to assess the organization's level of readiness and to examine the indicators that support the specific work-team design. The survey will assess the organization's performance in areas such as quality, profit, growth, production levels, turnover, absenteeism, accidents, labor disputes, and employee attitudes. The results of the survey must furnish the task force with enough information to establish the following:

◆ Work stations;

◆ Performance standards;

◆ Multiskilled workers;

◆ Coordination processes;

◆ Work interface and the accompanying coordination with managers, other work teams, suppliers, and customers; and

◆ A feedback system for the work-team members.

The task force may find that their organizational survey is hampered by the inability to collect and analyze data appropriately (the main barrier to success). Therefore, they must be prepared to use an alternative strategy: if the task force lacks expertise in research technology, it must seek the assistance of outside experts.

Data Analysis and Feedback. The purpose of this function is to analyze, evaluate, and give feedback on survey-collected data that will be used in the development of a work team designed especially for the organization. The information gathered by the task force is analyzed, developed into a set of recommendations, and shared with all stakeholders. In addition to establishing recommendations for work stations, performance standards, coordination systems, communication systems, and feedback systems, the task force must consider establishing the following support systems:

◆ Individual and team training in technical and human resource skills;

◆ Rewards (pay for knowledge and merit); and

◆ Systems for lateral career development and promotion.

However, because task-force members are, of course, members of the organization, their evaluations and recommendations may be prejudiced by their relationships with others, by political issues, or by self-interest. In addition, there can be negative repercussions to the survey itself, because the process of gathering data in this manner will stimulate discussion and reactions. Therefore, the task force must have as a member an impartial expert who can analyze the data objectively and can keep the group on track. The task force must be open and honest with all members of the organization about the purpose of the survey, and information and feedback must be collected and distributed in a timely manner.

Step 3: Implementation

The implementation phase is the final part of the process of education, planning, data collection, diagnosis, and evaluation. The purpose of the implementation phase is to plan, carry out, and evaluate the actions recommended by the task force.

Developing an Action Plan. Any plan for the implementation of a work-team system must consider the following:

♦ Location of work station(s);

♦ Who will comprise the work team;

♦ How work-team members will be selected;

♦ Which skills members will be required to possess;

♦ Which multifunctional skills will be considered desirable but optional;

♦ How the team will be managed;

♦ How results will be measured; and

♦ How rewards will be distributed.

In addition, the action plan must include time allotments for project start-up and evaluation.

The task force must take care to avoid pitfalls such as conducting the change process in a non-sequential manner or attempting to produce change too rapidly (too much, too soon, too fast). They may avoid these barriers to success by implementing the program in small chunks and by having realistic goals (e.g., by expecting some errors; by rewarding successes, however small; and by allowing time for teams to mature).

Implementing the Action Plan. During the implementation phase, the task force effects the changes necessary to activate the work teams. The implementation process begins with the training of work-team members in the technical and social skills needed to perform their multiple tasks and to interact smoothly with other team members. Team-building activities, which are also often part of this phase, can be conducted in classroom and laboratory settings and can evolve into on-the-job peer training. The final step in this phase is to ensure that a positive, supportive environment exists so that the work teams can function as planned.

Barriers to successful implementation can include a nonsupportive or hostile environment created by persons in the organization who are opposed to the work-team program and the failure to follow the program for implementation as planned. Task forces may need to cope with or circumvent barriers by seeing that top management becomes actively involved and by ensuring that the action plan is followed exactly as set down by the task force.

Evaluating the Action Plan. The evaluation step is essential to measure the program's progress, to gauge the effectiveness of the work-team design, and to discover any areas in the program or process that need to be adjusted. This step may be hampered by inadequate evaluation methods and by resistance to change. The task force must be prepared to deal with these barriers by ensuring that the evaluation method selected is suited to measure program progress and by maintaining a collaborative atmosphere to encourage the continued sharing of information.

Figure 6 depicts the strategies and action steps needed to implement a work-team system.

STRATEGIES FOR SUCCESS
- Empowerment
- Common Language
- Supportive Culture

ACTION STEPS FOR SUCCESS
Step 1: Education and Commitment
- Educate Top Management
- Educate Key Stakeholders

Step 2: Planning
- Form Task Force
- Organize and Conduct Survey
- Analyze Data
- Feedback Information

Step 3: Implementation
- Plan
- Implement
- Evaluate

Figure 6. Highlights of the Work-Team Implementation

CHAPTER SUMMARY

The successful implementation of a self-directed work team can aided by incorporating the three strategies of (1) empowering the work force, (2) developing a common language and (3) maintaining a supportive culture; and by following the three action steps of (1) education and commitment, (2) planning, and (3) implementation.

People, technology, the work environment, and the organizational culture must be managed effectively in order to implement a successful work-team system. Top management must be fully committed to the work-team concept and to supporting the change process.

The establishment of a work-team system can be successful only if management works closely with key stakeholders in the organization.

Finally, the implementation of a work-team system requires a great deal of time and effort on the part of both management and employees. Because of the high initial investment of finances and human resources, a total commitment to the work-team concept is required.

CONCLUSION

In a marketplace that is becoming more and more competitive, the organizations that survive will be those that eliminate waste, that increase productivity and quality, and that empower their work forces by developing collaborative work-team systems. To meet this challenge, organizations must be willing to re-evaluate their traditional perceptions of employees, the work design, and, most important, management.

This book has defined the three principles that govern work team systems (it must be semiautonomous and multiskilled and must have shared leadership) and has described the processes by which they function. Work teams have been examined with an analogy of the athletic team; five sports—baseball, football, basketball, volleyball, and tennis—have been compared to common work situations. The athletic-team analogies have demonstrated that form must follow function.

This book has discussed the benefits of increased productivity, improved service and product quality, increased employee morale, and reduced overhead, all of which can be linked to the use of work-team systems. A step-by-step process for work-team implementation was outlined: (1) empowering the work force, (2) developing a common language, and (3) maintaining a supportive culture. In addition, three accompanying action steps were presented: (1) education and commitment, (2) planning, and (3) implementation.

As the year 2000 approaches, organizations are becoming more group oriented; through the growing use of self-directed work teams, employees are beginning to have a more equal role in production and management processes. The greatest challenge that implementers of work-team systems face is finding a *champion* within the organization willing to pursue the vision and deal with the political ramifications created by attempts to change the traditional organizational structure. Implementers also must have the support of middle management and support staff when dealing with sweeping changes. Furthermore, because union-management relationships often are adversarial, it is important to have union representation in the planning and development of work-team systems from the very beginning. Without union support, great plans can quickly be halted. In short, managers must recognize that employees are resources and that they can make invaluable contributions to the production process. Involvement at all levels will increase an organization's competitive advantage. Ultimately, organizations must seek a balance between technology and human resources.

Appendix 1 outlines a training program whose purpose is to support and enhance the process of implementing a work-team system. Appendix 2 traces the influences of various management philosophies on self-directed work teams.

REFERENCES

Sherwood, J.J. (1988, Winter). Creating work cultures with competitive advantage. *Organizational Dynamics*, pp. 5-27.

APPENDIX 1

TRAINING OUTLINE FOR ESTABLISHING A WORK-TEAM SYSTEM

*It is critical for the facilitator to know
the priorities and learning goals of a
particular training event in order to
be able to specify them clearly and to
be able to keep the learning event
goal directed at all times.
(Pfeiffer & Ballew, 1988, p. 71)*

TRAINING TOP MANAGEMENT

I. Leadership

Objective: To educate top management in the basic elements of leadership to enable them to manage the transition to a work-team system.

Contents of the Session:

♦ Visioning
♦ Effective communication
♦ Trust
♦ Flexibility

II. Work-Team Concepts

Objective: To educate and to foster commitment on the part of top management to both the vision of and methods for implementing a work team system.

Contents of the Session:

♦ Empowerment
♦ Common language
♦ Supportive culture

TRAINING STAKEHOLDERS

I. Strategic Goals

Objective: To develop a support group of key stakeholders who understand and support the organization's strategic plan for establishing work-team systems.

Contents of the Session:

◆ Empowerment

◆ Common Language

◆ Supportive Culture

II. Team Building

Objective: To assist the key stakeholders in becoming an effective work group.

Contents of the Session:

◆ Empowerment

◆ Common Language

◆ Supportive Culture

III. Work-Team Concepts

Objective: To educate and to foster commitment on the part of key stakeholders to both the vision and the methods for implementing a work-team system.

Contents of the Session:

◆ Empowerment

◆ Common Language

♦ Supportive Culture

IV. Formation of a Task Force

Objective: To select a team of employees who are dedicated to the completion of a detailed analysis of the factors related to the establishment of a successful self-directed work-team system.

Contents of the Session:

♦ Decision Making
♦ Task-Force Selection

TRAINING THE TASK FORCE

I. Research Methodology

Objective: To teach task-force members methods of collecting, analyzing, and evaluating information.

Contents of the Session:

◆ Formulating a research design
◆ Sociotechnical job systems

TRAINING SUPERVISORS AND COORDINATORS

I. Work-Team Concepts

Objective: To educate and commit supervisors and coordinators to the vision and methods for implementing work-team systems.

Contents of the Session:

♦ Empowerment

♦ Common language

♦ Supportive culture

II. New Roles for Supervisors and Coordinators

Objective: To teach managers skills needed to supervise work-team systems.

Contents of the Session:

♦ Facilitation skills

♦ Problem-solving skills

♦ Consulting skills

TRAINING WORK-TEAM MEMBERS

I. Design of the Work Team

Objective: To educate work-team members in the principles that govern the operation of work teams.

Contents of the Session:

◆ Planning the work
◆ Doing the work
◆ Controlling the work
◆ Improving the work

II. Work-Team Management

Objective: To educate work-team members in methods for working with top management.

Contents of the Session:

◆ Personnel management
◆ Statistical process control
◆ Team dynamics
◆ Technical training as needed

REFERENCES

Pfeiffer, J.W., & Ballew, A.C. (1988). *Design skills in human resource development* (UA Training Technologies Series, vol. 6). San Diego, CA: University Associates.

APPENDIX 2

THE GENESIS OF WORK TEAMS

No matter how much work relies on technology for effective performance, it (work) does not exist independent of the social groups that bring it into existence and bestow it with meaning.
(Cummings & Srivastva, 1977, p. 22)

The use of work teams as a basic organizational building block is gaining greater popularity. Although the concept of work teams is not new, organizations are rediscovering that work teams contribute to a more satisfying and enriching work environment that can lead to increased productivity and quality and reduced costs (Lawler, 1986).

An appreciation of the work-team concept can be gained by a historical overview of predominant systems of management. Managerial philosophy has ranged from an emphasis on quality by craftspeople (in the preindustrial society) to an emphasis on statistical process control (SPC) methodology (in the postindustrial society). The period of time between preindustrial and post-industrial society can be divided into four management systems: *management by doing, management by directing, management by results,* and *management by method.* Figure 7 depicts a time line for each stage of management.

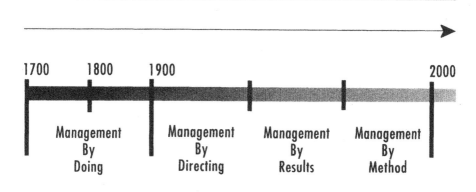

Figure 7. A Time Line of Managerial Philosophies

These philosophies are discussed from the perspective of key management and social theorists of the time, including commentary on management style, labor structure, reward systems, and work quality. It is hoped that, by gaining an understanding of the history of management philosophy, readers can better comprehend the forces contributing to the current need to establish work teams as the basic organization building block. Figure 8 shows the management learning process.

MANAGEMENT BY DOING

Preindustrial society was characterized by a production system based on the labor guild. Each master craftsman was a teacher and model who skillfully guided and trained his apprentices in a trade. Apprenticeships were rigidly controlled with extensive learning curves. However, once apprentices learned their crafts, they were able to plan, execute, control, and improve their own work.

This work system was based on the individual design and handcrafting of goods. The finished products were examples of the craftsman's artistic ability and were made to last over time. As a result, the craftsman's ability to produce high-quality products and services was often rewarded with both monetary and social recognition. Although each guild had specific standards for the goods they produced, general production standards were lacking.

Craft guilds were organized according to specific categories of skills and were governed by the following principles:

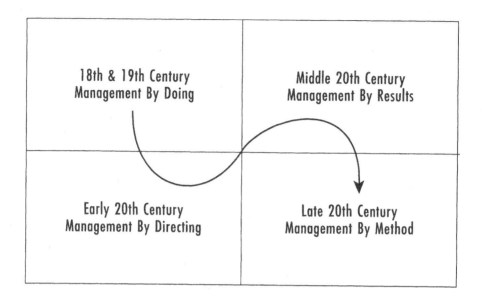

Figure 8. Management Learning Cycle

1. Each guild controlled how its particular skills were learned and used by a tightly defined membership.

2. Lengthy apprenticeships were required of those who aspired to membership in the guild.

3. Knowledge and craftsmanship were limited to guild members who would carry out the work with freedom and involvement (Cummings & Srivastva, 1977).

The management-by-doing method was similar to today's work-team structure. The production system involved small groups of people who collaborated to produce high-quality products. The teams had a high degree of control over quality, quantity, pricing, and design of their work.

The invention of the steam engine in 1782, however, resulted in new ways to mechanize the production process. This technological advancement precipitated a change in the system of work organization. The intimate feeling of the guild gave way to the impersonal factory in which workers no longer had control over the production process. In short, management by doing was no longer an effective management system.

MANAGEMENT BY DIRECTING

By the early twentieth century, the replacement of craft-oriented work by mechanized factories created a need for the development of *effective* methods for managing large organizations and *efficient* methods for increasing productivity. Max Weber, a German sociologist of this period, developed the concept of *bureaucracy*. A bureaucratic organizational structure facilitated the management of people in large organizations. The principles of bureaucracy are significant: they have served as the underpinnings of basic organizational structure throughout the twentieth century. Weber's (1930) principles of bureaucracy are as follows:

♦ A hierarchy of command based on rational/legal authority, which is established by the person's position in the hierarchy;

♦ Specialization and division of labor by functions (sales, production, engineering, and so on);

♦ Explicit system of procedures and rules to ensure adherence to "standard operating procedures" and to ensure that all employees are treated equally;

♦ A system of promotion and tenure based on skills and experience and measured by objective standards; and

♦ A system of communication within the organization and with the public characterized by written rules and the retention of decisions on public record.

These principles, which illustrate an inflexible and mechanical approach to organizational behavior, were an effective tool for the organization of labor and management during this period. Work was not expected or designed to be pleasant but simply to be productive. Workers were regarded as interchangeable and were expected to respond to the demands of the job unemotionally. The concept of bureaucracy, as presented by Weber, remains the guiding principle for many organizations today.

Another important contributor to the management-by-directing theory was Frederick Taylor, called the "father of scientific management," who developed a methodology for increasing the efficiency of the work force. He created a scientific management system that was designed to train workers in the one best way to do any given task. Taylor searched for ways to analyze tasks and to organize them into the most effective production process. Taylor's (1914) principles of scientific management were as follows:

♦ Time and motion studies, which determined precisely the most efficient methods for completing each task;

♦ A differential piece/rate system through which workers were rewarded for exceeding predetermined standards of performance established through time and motion studies;

♦ Selection, placement, and training of workers in the aforementioned systems by a line foreman and a planning department; and

♦ Standardization of cost systems, tools, and methods, thus creating a worker-machine system in which workers were interchangeable and easily replaced.

Taylor's system called for trained engineers to discover the most efficient methods of working. The common worker was not allowed to participate in planning or decision making. However, some may not realize that Taylor attempted to increase labor-management cooperation by reducing costs and by giving workers greater rewards. But management often denied workers' rewards by continually increasing production standards, thereby increasing the organization's profits at the expense of the workers. This led to the increasing dehumanization and disenfranchisement of the labor force, thus spurring an increase in the number of unions (Weisbord, 1987).

The development of Weber's bureaucratic principles and Taylor's scientific management theory contributed greatly to management by directing. *Control* was the key to this approach to management. The worker was considered an extension of the machine and was not viewed as separate from the production process. By breaking down production into its simplest components and detailing each task, jobs became highly standardized; they evolved into a narrowly defined set of physical tasks that were dictated solely by the pace of the machines (Hunsaker & Curtis, 1986). Workers were closely supervised and often could be fired without recourse. Management demanded high production but had little concern for workers' welfare. Extrinsic rewards (pay and benefits) were doled out, but the nature of the work denied workers the intrinsic sociological and psychological rewards that accompany satisfaction with one's job. Under management by directing, not only were the workers standardized but telephones were black, refrigerators were white, and bank checks were green. Even Henry Ford was reported to have commented that his customers could have any color automobile they wanted as long as it was black.

Management by directing met with mixed results. The quality of mass-produced items, like the Ford automobile, was only average, but customers could obtain them for an affordable price. There were few product styles available, workers felt alienated from both the production process and their employers, and management exhibited a flagrant lack of sympathy for workers' needs for self-respect, recognition, and self-direction.

Management by directing made its biggest contribution to the work-team concept through Taylor's principles of scientific management. Taylor's error was that he believed that only engineers and experts could plan and control the work; however, work teams today can manage all aspects of the production process.

MANAGEMENT BY RESULTS

By the middle of the twentieth century, the classic approach to management was looked upon as dehumanizing and overly simplistic. The beliefs that workers were basically lazy, motivated only by self-interest, and had to be kept in line were challenged by Elton Mayo and others during this period.

In 1924, Mayo studied the relationships between physical working conditions—lighting, temperature, and so on—and duration of work and worker productivity in his famous Hawthorne studies. The studies, which were conducted at the Western Electric Company's Hawthorne plant near Chicago, produced interesting results. Mayo found that workers in his experimental group (whose opinions were valued) became more productive regardless of the changes in their physical environments. Mayo concluded that the presence or absence of human factors such as self-respect, recognition, and self-direction had a greater influence on productivity (Mayo, 1933). The results of Mayo's studies marked the beginning of the behavioral-science investigation directed at improving productivity and organizational effectiveness by emphasizing the critical human factors.

Two other social scientists who contributed to the management-by-results movement were Abraham Maslow (1943) and Douglas McGregor (1960). Maslow created a model depicting the relationship between human motivation and performance. His insights provided a framework for management to use when attempting to motivate their employees to be more productive.

Maslow's model (Figure 9) included five levels of human needs:

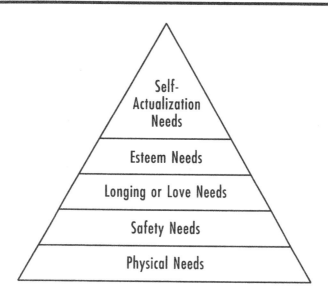

Figure 9. Maslow's Hierarchy of Human Needs

1. *Physical needs:* food, water, shelter, clothing, sex.

2. *Safety needs:* predictability, security, freedom from physical harm.

3. *Longing or love needs:* nurturing, acceptance, respect, meaningful interpersonal relationships.

4. *Esteem needs:* status, feelings of self-worth through outside recognition and appreciation.

5. *Self-actualization needs:* the ability and opportunity to develop latent capabilities and to realize one's maximum potential.

Although Maslow's theory of motivation has been oversimplified by managers who assumed that people can be moved up the hierarchy without taking their personal and social circumstances into consideration, it remains a useful model for a basic understanding of human motivation.

Douglas McGregor, who was influenced by Maslow's thinking, presented two sets of assumptions about motivation in his book, *The Human Side of Enterprise.* He proposed that a manager's assumptions about human motivation influences his or her managerial style. McGregor called these contrasting sets of assumptions *Theory X* and *Theory Y.* McGregor stated that a person who subscribes to the Theory X assumptions believes that:

◆ Most people are passive and indolent and work as little as possible;

◆ People dislike responsibility and lack ambition; they would rather follow than lead; and

◆ People are self-centered and thus are indifferent to organizational needs and by nature are resistant to change.

McGregor stated that managers who operate under Theory X assumptions tend to persuade, reward, punish, and control their employees in order to obtain high productivity. In contrast, McGregor believed that a person who subscribes to Theory Y assumptions believes that:

◆ People are not passive or indifferent to organizational needs by nature; however, they often become that way because of their experiences on the job; and

♦ People want responsibility and are capable of exercising self-direction and self-control with regard to work tasks.

McGregor believed that managers who subscribe to Theory Y beliefs tend to organize the work so that employees will achieve their personal goals by reaching the organization's objectives.

By the middle of the twentieth century, the research by Mayo, Maslow, McGregor, and others had had a significant impact on management philosophy. Although organizations did not capitalize on the new ideas to the fullest, they did begin to raise employees' status and to understand the connections between human factors and productivity.

Management philosophy during this period was also influenced by Kurt Lewin, a social scientist who focused on organizational structure and systems theory rather than on motivational factors. Lewin, known as the "father of group dynamics," realized as early as 1920 that Taylor's principles of scientific management were incomplete. Lewin addressed issues of both productivity and individual needs, as well as the needs of the organization. He pioneered the concept and theory of planned change. Lewin was especially interested in social change; he believed that research techniques could play an important role in the generation, direction, and implementation of change efforts. He believed that knowledge gained could be properly used only after a process of analysis, information gathering, action planning, action, and evaluation (Weisbord, 1987).

In addition, Lewin sought to establish that psychology is a formal science based on principles that can explain and describe human behavior. He combined scientific management with democratic values, thereby developing the concept of *participatory management.* In contrast to Taylor's belief that only technically trained engineers could increase production, Lewin believed that workers could improve their skills by learning from everyday work situations, thus adding a new dimension to the organizational quest for improved productivity (Lewin, 1951).

Management by results, a theory that is still used, is based on a production system of high automation and planned obsolescence with an emphasis on meeting production goals. Product quality is not a high priority; products are often produced with a high degree of waste and rework. Quality control is performed by inspectors who weed out defective products at the end of the production line.

Management-by-results theory recognized the need to satisfy the human factors, which it attempted to do through health plans, retirement plans, safer working conditions, incentive pay, paid vacations, and profit-sharing plans. These benefits rewarded employees who demonstrated a high degree of loyalty, who stayed with their organizations, and who conformed to their organizations' standards. These benefits did *not* reward quality consciousness, innovative thinking, or problem solving. For example, employees earned paid vacation time in accordance with their years with the organization, not by the amount of their contributions to organizational productivity.

Because of politics, job protection, and labor-management disputes, management was often unwilling or unable to put the principles of management by results into practice. This often resulted in a divided and competitive relationship between management and employees. Contract negotiations, labor disputes, and strikes contributed to stressful relationships between employees and management and resulted in poor-quality products and lowered productivity. It is easy to understand why, following a long and bitter strike, employees could have difficulty re-identifying with their organization and its products.

MANAGEMENT BY METHOD

Many of the principles of today's self-directed work teams were adapted from the theories of Maslow, McGregor, Mayo, and Lewin. By the middle of the twentieth century, scientifically based management principles and an emphasis on a humanistic work environment contributed to the concept of *sociotechnical systems.*

Sociotechnical systems practitioners sought to enlarge employees' understanding of the social and economic consequences of their work. Employees were encouraged to develop their skills in order to obtain better results. The *system,* rather than individual tasks, became the unit of study. Management theory began to focus on the work group and to call for a sense of responsibility from work-group members.

Eric Trist, who coined the term "sociotechnical systems," observed that the interaction of people (the social system) with tools and techniques (the technical system) results from *choice,* not *chance* (Weisbord, 1987). The objective of sociotechnical systems theory was to match human and technical systems in order to achieve a higher degree of quality, quantity, and employee satisfaction. Studies of the introduction of automated technology into industries such as electronics, textiles, and mining indicated that tasks such as job assignment, production methods, scheduling, and employee compensation were best achieved with the use of team-centered decisions. Trist, along with other researchers, demonstrated that work groups with the power to manage themselves and to make decisions are more productive and are better able to cope with change in the work place.

Sociotechnical systems theory was furthered by W. Edwards Deming's scientific methodology that he called *statistical process control* (SPC). Deming, known as the "father of the new industrial age," realized the importance of quality and of the application of statistical thinking to the production process. His approach was data based, objective, and scientific, relying on statistics and logic (Scholtes, 1988).

According to Deming, paying attention to work processes at the beginning of the production cycle results in lowered product costs and increased productivity. Furthermore, the higher level of quality achieved through the use of SPC will improve the organization's competitive position. To make this happen, organizations must determine their customers' needs and expectations and develop a system of values, policies, and practices. As Modic (1988, p. 23) put it, "Quality on the shop floor can be no better than the intent of management which is made in the board room."

Much of Deming's philosophy is drawn from the tradition of humanistic management and from sociotechnical principles. He believed that all employees are motivated by the opportunity to work with pride; therefore, they must be involved in the development, refinement, and control of systems and methods in order to maintain and increase quality. Deming advised organizations that replacement of time standards and work quotas with effective leadership and high quality would lead to increased productivity and satisfied, confident employees (Modic, 1988).

Deming's philosophy of management can be expressed in the following fourteen points, and his chain reaction is illustrated in Figure 10 (Scholtes, 1988).

1. Create consistency of purpose in order to improve product and service quality.

Figure 10. Deming's Chain Reaction

2. Adopt the philosophy of "leadership for change."

3. Cease dependence on end-of-the-line quality inspections. Improve the production process instead.

4. End the practice of awarding one's business solely on the basis of cost; rather, reduce costs by working with a single supplier.

5. Strive always to improve every process for planning, production, and service. Remember that quality must be built in at the design stage.

6. Institute on-the-job training. A manager's primary role is that of trainer.

7. Adopt and institute leadership. The manager's job is not to supervise; it is to lead.

8. Drive out fear.

9. Break down barriers between staff areas; teamwork is critical.

10. Eliminate slogans, exhortations, and targets for the work force. The primary responsibility for improving the system belongs to management.

11. Eliminate numerical quotas for the work force and numerical goals for management.

12. Remove the barriers that rob people of their pride in workmanship, including the annual rating or merit system.

13. Institute a vigorous program of education and self-improvement for everyone in the organization.

14. Put everybody in the company to work on accomplishing the desired transformation.

By following Deming's fourteen principles, organizations will be implementing management by method. Through SPC, management works closely with employees to develop ways of improving the organization. Management by method is the most effective management approach for today's information age. Production methods are based on advanced technology, and products are built to last. The emphasis on SPC, coupled with increased employee involvement, will ensure a higher quality of products and services. By collaborating with and empowering the work force, management and employees will become true partners. The rewards of using this system are both extrinsic (monetary gain and benefits) and intrinsic (job satisfaction, group involvement, and decision making). If management by method is correctly incorporated into organizations, self-directed work teams will prove to be the single most effective tool for organizing, motivating, and training people.

Figure 11 illustrates the differences in the four management systems.

SUMMARY

Work-team principles have evolved from aspects of management systems that have proven most effective over time. Like the small-group production system characteristic of management by doing, today's work teams provide employees with the opportunity to be social, to be creative, and to earn money. The theory behind self-directed work teams also incorporates Taylor's principles of scientific management; management-by-directing theory; the theories of Maslow, McGregor, Mayo, and Lewin; and is organized according to Trist's sociotechnical systems theory. Work teams' output (goods and

Management System	Production Method	Management Method	Labor Structure	Individual Reward	Quality of Work
Management by DOING (18th and 19th Centuries)	Individual produces a product that is built to last	Modeling	Tightly defined with lengthy apprenticeships	Socially and psychologically satisfying	High quality design; non-standardized; individually inspected
Management by DIRECTING (Early 20th Century)	Mass production; built to wear	Controlling	Extension of the machine	Socially and psychologically lacking	Average quality; standardized; inspected by supervision
Management by RESULTS (Middle 20th Century)	Automation; planned obsolescence	Goal setting	Highly divided; unionized; stressful	Premium on higher thinking skills; physical labor minimized	Average quality; standardized; quality control inspected
Management by METHOD (Late 20th Century)	Information; high-speed technology; built to last	Collaboration	Partnership with management	Socially and psychologically balanced	High quality; statistical quality control; inspected by work groups

Figure 11. Historical Relationship Between Methods of Production and Management and Labor

services) is made better and more productive through management's application of Deming's fourteen points.

REFERENCES

Cummings, C.G., & Srivastva, S. (1977). *Management of work*. San Diego, CA: University Associates.

Hunsaker, P.L., & Curtis, W. (1986). *Managing organizational behavior*. Reading, MA: Addison-Wesley.

Lawler, E.E. (1986). *High involvement management*. San Francisco: Jossey-Bass.

Lewin, K. (1951). *Field theory in social sciences*. New York: Harper & Row.

Maslow, A.H. (1943). A theory of human motivation. *Psychological Review, 50,* 370-396.

Mayo, E. (1933). *The human problems of an industrial civilization*. New York: Macmillan.

McGregor, D. (1960). *The human side of enterprise*. New York: McGraw-Hill.

Modic, S.J. (1988, June). What makes Deming run? *Industry Week,* pp. 21-26.

Scholtes, P.R. (1988). *The team handbook*. Madison, WI: Joiner Associates.

Taylor, F.W. (1914). *Principles of scientific management*. New York: Harper & Row.

Weber, M. (1930). *The Protestant ethic and the spirit of capitalism* (F. Parsons, Trans.). New York: Scribner. (Original work published 1904)

Weisbord, M.R. (1987). *Productive workplaces*. San Francisco: Jossey-Bass.

Colophon

Editors: Jennifer O. Bryant and Marian K. Prokop

Cover Design and Chapter-Opener Illustrations:
Susan Odelson

Cover and Chapter 2 Illustrations:
Janet Colby

Interior Design: Paul Bond

Page Composition: Judy Whalen

Camera-ready art was prepared by University Associates.
The text is twelve on fourteen New Century Schoolbook
and the headings are Futura Medium Bold.